Beautiful Disasters

by

ELABETH COONEY

Wild Ink Publishing LLC

A Wild Ink Publishing Publishing Original
wild-ink-publishing.com

Copyright © 2023 Elabeth Cooney
Edited by Brittany McMunn
Cover Design and Layout by Abigail Wild

ISBN: 978-1-958531-56-3

This book is dedicated to all who lost their
battle with mental health/addiction
in some form.

As well as Edward, Patrick, Hans, and to PPI
(Pennsylvania Psychiatric Institute) for putting
up with me so much as a teenager.

TABLE OF CONTENTS

DYSPHORIA

the monster in me
fights to be free
he wants out of his cell
and into the ways of being me
he wants to be me
his name is dysphoria
he wants to become alive
he wants to take over this poor girl's life
he wants to be the only one
he wants to be the king of kings
dysphoria runs as fast as he can
dysphoria wants to have a plan
dysphoria needs to kill himself
because he can't become alive and well
dysphoria is sick
he must die
and to hell
he goes, Goodbye

TEARDROPS

memory lane
here we go
down to the water
my tears they fall.

DISSOCIATION

down to the waterfall
through the trees
this is where you will find me
you will find me standing there
glancing in the mirror with self-hate
no idea where to go
what is life?
is it a joke?
a lie?
a dream?
a fairytale?
what if life was a movie scene
And the movies were life?
what if this is what I believe?
will I be called crazy
for the cuts on my skin
or will I be loved
it's all just a scene in a play
please don't go
my love
I'm waiting
impatiently, I stand under the waterfall
through the trees
I stand here
next to you in glee

BROKEN

weeping willows and beautiful lies
the weather
it's a storm
what shall they say
shall they stab or grin
will they lie or love
who will know
it's a big world
we're all alike
but we're also different
who knows what life is
maybe it's a fairytale
who knows what love is
maybe it's a living hell

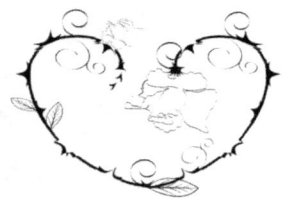

START OVER AGAIN

why won't the voices stop?
why can't my life go back to normal?
why can't this depression go away?
because of course it has to stay
but now you leave
I say my goodbyes
my frail body breaks
but then revives
as we grow old
we come and go
as we get wiser
we grow up too
yes, I will grow over you
and I will get older too
one day at finkenbinder
I have that reminder the memories repeat
why did I come back to this town?
was it to watch how the years fly by?
was it to find the key to my goals?
I shall one day leave,
and one day return
with my last nerve
I say goodbye
to my family and friends
in this small town
it's time to move up
and time to grow up
as I stand at the airport with my poor mother
on the plane to a new chapter

a new life
a new book
we fly back to the past
but it will be ok, darling, yes it will
I will go my own way
I will stay strong and say goodbye one day
but not for long
cause deep in my heart there you will be
deep in my heart lies the memories
we all grow old and pass one day
but never take your life
'cause that's the wrong way
and just one more thing to say
I love you to pieces
But this is how it works
here's the plan,
here's the pain,
here's the love,
and here's the broken
I will be back, I promise;
even if it's not for weeks,
for months,
for years.
I will return,
just be patient, my love.
As I awaken from this dream
I say "What happened"?
Oh honey, it was all a dream
you'll be fine;

and since that night
since that dream
I was fine.

SUICIDE

Can't live this life no more.
Can't take the pain no more.
They say death isn't the answer,
But the only true escape is suicide.
Suicide shall bring me glee,
'cause the world will say goodbye to poor little me.
Goodbye, my love. Hello to hell.
I must go, I can't take the emotions life has given.
I must leave you behind,
I'm sorry.
Stay strong,
it's for the best of our kind.

DARKNESS

But the darkness in her eyes was nothing but a mistake.
The darkness she lived with was all a fake.
The darkness,
the pain,
the dreadful lies she told.
Darling, you're hurt,
we know.
Darling, it'll be okay,
which you do not know.
Darling, one day
we will all fly across the sky.
Catching our dreams up above the clouds;
above the moons and stars,
above all of the universe,
and above all;
no worries, just joy.
Just remember, my love,
you'll be okay one day.
One day the worries will escape,
and there will be no memory of pain.
Because all you will fear isn't anywhere near shame,
all you will know is life is a blessing,
a gift from above;
and all you will do is know how to love.
Love yourself, your neighbor, your foe,
love all that you may ever know.
Love for infinite,
for then hate shall burst to flames;
the world will become a happy place.

Finally, we are all at peace with ourselves,
but the question is when?
When will we all be okay?
When will the fighting, the fury, and the jealousy escape?
When will we all know it is fine to live our lives?
When will we know stepping outside of our house
isn't stepping into death's door
but stepping into a world filled with beauty, not horror and
gore?
When will there be no more worries, just happiness with-
out pain?
When will we be unafraid to talk with our enemy?
When will we not feel the need to cause our own bleeding?
When will we never fear how much money we own or
gain?
Someday, my love, the world will be great.
Someday, we will all be safe.
And in another fairytale, another once upon a time.
That's all this is now,
it's just a dream to become the truth to our world.
Our lives shall finally become renewed.

BREAK THE CYCLE

my life is a movie
your love is a dream
and all I can wonder
is how can you be
in love with me
in love with him
in love with all of them.
how is it alright
for you to play with the hearts of all
but say you've been played too?
how can you love me if you don't even love you?
how can I make you happy if it's all a lie?
how could you leave me behind
in a world filled with darkness and broken dreams?
how could you do this?
how did you ever love me?
did you ever love me
or was it all another scene?
a scene in a movie called life
or was it another dream?
do you wake up to feeling clean?
because that dream wiped away those feelings
only to bring on another whisper of butterflies in my
stomach
for another boy or girl
another crush is brewing within me
and the cycle moves on
and viciously continues for eternity
you fall

you break
and you realize the mistakes you've made
throughout your life
your life, the dream
it was all just another scream
for help
a scream
for love
and tonight that cycle will break
and darling I'll stay with you for eternity
no more breaking hearts
no more puppy love
just whispers of truth
and screams of joy
because you and I will survive this time
and this time the cycle is broken
and this love lasts for eternity
so you and I will never die
because our love is so long it could survive a bullet in the
heart
and it did
and it will
and I will always forgive you
i will always love you
and happily ever afters
aren't always a dream
because sometimes they become reality.

THINKING OUT LOUD

what is love without trust but loyalty?
fear but constantly being reminded love is real?
what is it like to be told constantly you are cared for and
loved, but all your mind does is say otherwise
and your heart believes every single word they say?
how does it feel to be nothing but a broken masterpiece?
it's like when the wind blows from the north but it
makes you happy
even though it's cold and you don't want to freeze
but at the same time, death is the only thing you can
think of
what is life about?
they say it's about finding the good in the bad
the light in the darkness
and it's funny how a broken thing can be turned into a
beautiful casualty
people say life is good
I like to think life is dark
but even though the light makes me sad
it's the darkness in the night that brings me joy
I still survive and every day I wonder
what would it be like if every day had thunder?
if every day was rainy and cold
and every night you wanted someone to hold
but what if every night you did have someone to hold?
and even after every miserable, long sad day
you could look forward to the evening
because you could hold the one person you're craving
the one you want to feel your body against

the one you want to share that feeling
and then you wonder if you even want to live
because yes, they all love you, they do
and even though your heart believes it too
your mind is still fucked up
and people ask what it's like to live your life
and all you respond with is luck
because even if you feel like it wasn't a blessing
that you survived that fall
that you survived that heartbreak
even though you wish it didn't fail
you know deep down that maybe it was amazing you lived
and your body didn't collapse
maybe it's a miracle
you didn't have a heart attack
the level of poison in your veins
didn't kill you
but instead taught you strength
strength is what you have
not just physically
emotionally too
and the fact you survived that night makes you wonder
"am i worth it too"?
are you worth it like everyone says you are?
or is this just another dream that will become far
away in my mind
a dream I will forget
what if life is nothing but
me looking back on my

regrets I did in my past life
what if this world isn't real?
what if it's all a dream
and life
is nothing but a broken piece
of the hearts
of the ones who fell?
for the one
they thought would last forever
but then
they died
and we all committed suicide
and now what we do is
look back at our past life
from heaven or hell
wherever we are now
we are trying
again
at life
at our emotions
trying again to
not fail
but to survive and
fix what was broken
maybe life is about fixing the past
and making sure life isn't going to last
forever as
a living hell
and maybe all we need to do is
get well

UNTITLED

stress is a beautiful thing but also deadly and dark
but darkness is beauty
and beauty is mine
I am beautiful
and one-of-a-kind
life is strange
who would have thought it'd be true
that you love me
and I love you too
but who would think that even with love everlasting
I just want to be alone
because God it is so relaxing
It's calming here in my bed asleep
no worries
no thoughts
only sweet dreams
no one to care for
no one to be scared of
now all I can do is think of what a life I have lived
I was alone
But loneliness is happy
and all I can do
is never make your heartbeat
for me
and not for yourself
don't stay alive for me
be sure to get some help
but in all reality, you don't need help
all you need to do is love yourself

don't rely on others
only you
because one day when you have nothing left
you will still be you
you still will be alive
and you can't live without pride
and if you don't love yourself
you just wanna die
and all you can do is think
life is no fun
but all I can do and think is
how exciting it is to watch the sun
set into the night sky
Because the night is the place I always thrive
And in the day I usually sleep
but once it's night
all I can do is creep
outside
into the dark
I love the night
I love the mark you made on my skin
when you told me you loved me
But that was a lie, not a sin
all you did was feel pity and so
you were so kind you could not say no
all you could do is fake your love
and all I can do is believe I am above
the others and all the feelings
and how I feel is beyond this world of living

and now all I want to do is live
because you love me
never mind you're a kid
you're immature and don't know how to act
polite
sweet
fuck that
you don't know how to react
how to become mature
you will never know
maybe you will one day realize I am not that
hoe
or a wreck
Maybe I'm the best
maybe I am better off than the rest
of your friends
the ones you really hate
you say you have no friends
you liar
you cheat
all you can do is think
of yourself
of your life
and all I can do is say goodbye

I HATE YOU

As he tells him he loves him
And is told the same
And then he realized it's just a game
Nothing is real
No one truly loves
If he hung himself today
They would all gather around
They would laugh
Not cry
They would cheer and tell him
Do it!
Die!
He would do it and he would complete
What he had been trying to do for years
But he was too weak
He thought they all cared
He really started to believe it
But then one day
He knew he couldn't stand
The knives called words
The bullets called love
They all say it's ok
But really it is not
And I try to express myself
But I really can't
Goodbye
It's the end
Of a beautiful life
In the body of a girl

The boy who isn't really correct
He never felt right
Always knew it was wrong
Life wasn't worth it
Unless you had it all
If you had friends
Family
Fame
Money
People who cared
Then maybe it was okay to live and have a love affair
Maybe it would be okay if I didn't really care
But I do
And I will
But will you?
No
Never
Never will you dare
To actually love me the way I did
Who ever cared?
Not you
Not him
You wonder why you have no friends
It's because you're a selfish, lying dick
You say you have no friends, so everyone comes to you
You want attention
It's all you crave
And now all I can do is say
Go away

Go to hell
Cause that's how I felt when you said you loved me
But you didn't
You hate
You love, but you hate
Because you don't give a fuck
You wouldn't care if I did go to the tree
And I hung myself
If anyone was to care
You'd be the last
You'd say you felt like it was all your fault
Like you're the reason that I am dead
But then within a few months, you would feel relief
Because you know that you don't have to deal with me
And you can move on to a new boy
A new life
You can hurt them as well
And never remember how much I loved
How much I cared
But who the fuck cares
Why am I here?

RED CHEEKS

my cheeks turn red thinking of the memories with me and you
just thinking of the beautiful nights
and how amazing it feels to have you by my side
my heart begins to warm when I think about
how beautiful you are
and how perfection may exist in you through my eyes
for you are so fantastic
and you are mine, just mine
my body tingles and I feel like I shall float
when we look into each other's eyes
and you can't help but kiss me
and I can't help but smile while I lay here and I daydream
about all of our nights ahead
and I blush at the thought of you right next to me in bed
as you kiss my neck
and I sigh with joy
and I whisper I love you
and you say the same in return
I sit here on my couch blushing,
waiting for you to come back
for another night of laughter and happiness
and a future of forever
because you are mine
and I am yours

SURVIVED

Stay with me
The emotions are usually out of control
But I finally feel in control
I feel like I can breathe
So, please stay with me for stability
Now I can breathe again
Don't go, stay with me
Because this new feeling I've felt many years ago
Nostalgic and old
It's happiness, the joy has returned
The demons are dying
I'll be ok
I am ok
I am reviving
My happiness is alive
I am alive
And what a beautiful life to have survived
I look around
I feel joy and true confidence
It's so amazing
I'm glad
The demons are gone
They have lost the fight
I have survived

WHY

why is my mood the color of my shirt?
the color of the sky?
the color of when I hurt?
why am I so angry?
so red like the color of the blood falling from my enemies
and my wrists
why are the colors so meaningful all around?
why are they so deep like the ocean and my heart's beat?
why are such things so alike when they're such opposites?
how come things are so angry but so happy, and why is your
smile lopsided?
why do good things end and why are some sad things so
beautiful?
why is it that we question it, rather than enjoy what we have,
and play with our brains full of knowledge
our hearts full of joy
our spirits filled with courage
and our stomachs filled with butterflies from our lover's kiss.

FOR COLIN

even if you think no one loves you, everyone comes running
back when you're gone.
we miss you so much
the whole town cries
even the clouds weep
we never wanted you to leave
we never truly thought you would go
our hearts pour with sadness and love
and God we wish we could have another go
please know we loved you so dearly
even if you're not here
we miss your talk of the military
and we miss your long hair and cheer
you could always become happy
even if you didn't see
please, come back to us Raymond, for then our emotions will
be at ease.
april 28th, 2018 is the date I will never forget
my old friend passed and my good friends fainted
and I almost couldn't grasp
reality
the thought of you gone
the true world we have around us
now remember love, even though you are gone
you are now at peace with yourself
so rest easy, my sweet Colin
we miss you so much

and we want you more than you may have known.
rest in peace, we will miss your kind heart, even if you
thought it was cold.

2/16/19

cigarettes and daydreams
cigarettes and smoke rings
here I am
here I stand today.

PAINS OF ALL KINDS, MY PARENTAL GUARDIANS

do you ever just panic and run for the stars?
or the moon, or the sun?
or you're inspired by your father from a lifetime
before you?
thunder hawk.
or you're inspired by your mother, right in front
of you?
fear overcomes you
and then mania becomes an emotion
thank you, my beauty. I love you, sweet pain.
panic.
fear.
sorrow.
guilt.
extreme external relief, I cry.
oh well.

TODAY

today's a day of new beginnings
letting go
of the past beings
let in the fresh air
let go of the old love
let in the new joy
the real joy
let the smiles release upon my face
let the tears flow in a different way
let the joy come
let the tears flood to peace
let the peace come to me

UNTITLED 3

I dreamt about you again tonight
I can't fight this feeling anymore
you make me feel like I wanna die
I regret the things I did
I'm sorry, my love
I can't handle this pain
I'll cut so deep for you
I wanted us to rule a kingdom
you would be the king
I'd be the queen
I can't fight this feeling anymore
fuck this feeling
you're overtaking my mind
I'm obsessed
I'm addicted
to your love
why can't I get you off my mind?

ADDICTED

I can still smell you
I can see you smoking your cigarettes with bliss
I can see you through my mind
I miss your scent
your eyes
your touch
your laugh
You're driving me crazy, boy
crazier than before
I feel like I need to go to rehab
because your love is the strongest drug in store

BROKE

I can't laugh anymore
I can only fall apart
but of course, you can
but you left me in the dark
you tore me to pieces
Baby, why did you go
don't leave me broken, honey
all these crushes are here now, they have to go
why did you do this, lovely
I wanted you for life
your beautiful blue eyes haunt me
every day and every night

BROKEN LOVE

I like to imagine you miss me even though you hate me
I like to imagine you're jealous because I took your virginity
I like to imagine you're angry because I'm marrying her
and not you
you're mad he's the dad
when he's supposed to be your best friend
he was my next partner
my possible future husband
you wonder
why did I break you
It's because I fucking
hate you
and your psychotic brain cells
you're stupid
you're lame
go die in a ditch
I'll be the one to blame

Crisis

help me
I need an ambulance
I have a broken heart
but I don't think it can be fixed
because you tore it apart
help me
it's a crisis
I'm going crazy without you

PLAN OF THE GODS

God, is this the right decision?
Dad, why aren't you here?
Why did you have to go?
Why couldn't you live to see your daughter become a
mama?
Why couldn't you live to see your grandbaby?
Father, father I need you now.
I need you, Lord. Help me.
I need my dad.
I don't even know if this kid will have one.
Sadness overcomes me
My stomach swells
This baby is lonely for their daddy
For their granddaddy as well
Mama, what happened?
Where did he go?
His sadness overwhelmed him and heaven took him as
an angel of their own.
Don't worry, it won't happen to you unless you allow it.
You'll understand one day, but you're too young now.
Baby boy, baby girl.
You're only a month, you've got eight more.
Only a few hours til I know for sure
If your existence is real
It will explain the puking
The cravings
The crying
The screaming
The bloating

Why so young?
I don't know, but we don't question God's plan.

FATHER

The cold air of a ghost I feel
When I hear the harmonica
A smile upon my face
Because you saved my life
Thank you, Lord
He saved my life
Thank you, dad
You saved me once more
I'm sorry I couldn't save you
I guess this is your apology
I forgive you

HEARTBREAK SEASON

Its heartbreak season
Hearts shatter here and there
It's time to tell those you love them
Before you get torn apart

GOODBYE ALMOST LOVER

Why do I still yearn for you
Why do I still need you
Why do I still cry every night begging for you to return?
All you did was cheat me
And used me for love
And I am not a fool
But only a fool for your touch
My spirit breaks when I see her
I can't stand to see you anymore
I'm sorry, but you broke our friendship
Goodbye, my almost lover
I hope she was worth it

INFECTION

I feel like the infection won't go away
The depression
The scars
The puss on my skin
I'm dizzy because no doctor can find a cure
Why the hell won't it all disintegrate
Why do I have to feel this way
I ache
I cry
I sleep all day and night
What is wrong with me
I feel like I am dying
Rotting away

BROKEN HEARTS MENDED

the sun has come and gone
my skin has been sliced
my mind has broken
I can not function
without you here to hold
hold me, darling
squeeze me tight
for the anxiety is calling
and it's giving me a fright
I don't know how much longer I can conquer my fears
but I know soon you will be with me, my dear
you will mend my beating heart
and push my hair behind my ears
you will kiss me goodnight
and say I wish I could always be here
by your side
in your arms
starring into your beautiful green eyes

LEFT BEHIND

left behind
broken inside
melting away
can not contain my insanity
can not stand the sight of me
here I go again
going insane
I'm sorry, my love
maybe this time I'll behave

EMOTIONS EMERGING

we're gonna die young
take it as it is
emotions emerge
fuck life
I give what I learn
baby, I love you to pieces
don't leave me. I love you

TRUE LOVE

the world slows down when I'm around you
everything feels so right
I lay near you
and feel your heart pound
it beats to the rhythm of my own pulse
we move in time together
just the right pace
your love is tender and kind
our auras vibrate
perfectly entwined

8/19/2020

I still smell your scent beside my bed
I still worry if you responded too late
I still know this relationship isn't right
but I don't know if there's anyone else i could love like I
love you
I'm sorry, I'm a mess
anxiety gets to me all the time
I'm sorry, I love you
I'm sorry, I can be selfish
but if this is goodbye, let me know
if I'm being dramatic, whisper to me sweet dreams
because I can't sleep with this fear in my brain

FINAL GOODBYE

one final farewell parade to ease my anxiety
good riddance it was finally goodbye for eternity
you cursed my brain without any witchcraft, just misery
I think of you now and then
I pray you're well
even though you don't believe in any of that
darling, we will be okay
we were made to be apart
now I pray you don't take your razor blades
and tear your arms apart
it'll be okay, sweetie
no matter how much you regret ditching me in a hole
I'll fly high with my achievements
while you mow along with your blasphemy of goals

MONSTER

darling, you sometimes still appear in my mind
sometimes you still dance along my thoughts
but I know I don't step foot on your brain stems
and, my love, I'm glad you've vanished
you were killing me inside
I can't believe you're still gone
I honestly can't believe the monster you became
but you'll be okay
and so will I

YOU

no more tears to cry, only while I sleep and dream
of you
for it feels so real
it feels like I can grasp your attention
only to awaken to nothing but an unopened
message

THE RACES

I died again
tonight I died once again
I kissed her lips
her breath smelled of alcohol
we laughed and watched the cars race along the track
then he came along
he was the worst imaginable
I sat alone on the third floor
watching her being torn apart
I watched him pretend to make love to her
only to break her heart
I shake in fear worried I'll be next
I want to cry
but I know there's no more tears left
I cry to my mother in the car on the way home
home to safety
far away from the trauma
never again will I visit State Street
not without anger
sadness
or a worried frown
I cry for my partner in crime
My best friend
my lover
I would do anything for her
but the alcohol on her breath cost her soul
her sanity
her virginity
now I cry, regretting that night deeply

I should have run to my firey-haired lover
working for the cars racing through the clay track
I pray to the Gods I will run to him for help next
but for now, I have my lonesome mother
who would give her life for mine

DEATH 6/4/21

all cut up
I feel like death
sometimes I wonder why I get so depressed
but I don't ask why
I let the tears fly by
if there's any left to cry
I look at the stars and moon
and I see how beautiful the sky blooms
I cry once more and wipe my tears
then I realize life is beautiful
I have no fear
I am strong but sometimes weak
I am a powerful
but sometimes only a survivor
I will some day make it
I'll shoot for those stars
don't you worry, darling
we are who we are

FOR AMY

I dreamt of you again last night, darling
high as a kite
I fell asleep with a white-powdered nose
we fought demons
I held you close
I miss you, my friend
it felt so real
I pray I see you again
I pray you feel good

ELEPHANT IN THE ROOM

The elephant in the room is puking the guts and hearts
of our past
We are digesting the love of our present and future
Just for the elephant to be immune to this love
Because this love is whole, not broken
And I will love thee like hot chocolate and bubble baths
While you love me like the stars and dopamine
Together we are whole
And the elephant shall starve for there is no more torn
hearts of ours
The elephant in the room will die off
And it won't matter anymore
For it will be you and I for eternity

SOCIETY

I spy through the looking glass
I see the world around me
I see the tears running down their dark faces
and the way they can't see their beauty
Behind the looking glass, I stand against the hatred of
the children
I stand against the ones who intrude on my privacy
I stand against the ones who do not believe in me
I once was the girl with the tears rolling down her face
But I know if it wasn't for the color of my skin, I would
not be truly
Free
Free, from
hatred,
racism,
violence,
lynching.
And one day, free at last they will be.
The children go to school saying, "goodbye Mommy"
They do not know if they will return that day
Because of the way they shoot their AR-15s
If it wasn't for the computer I learned on,
I wouldn't be alive,
Breathing
Without sorrow
But still, I cry in pain,
The loss of my father due to the epidemic of sorrow
and insanity
The society says we must keep our guns, we must keep

our pills, we must keep our sorrow and sanity.
But we also say
we want world peace
But to be joyous, we must keep our children safe
Our rehabs open
Our mental health care steady
But hold on,
Am I ready for the war on equality, drugs, mental illness,
and race?
Yes, I am ready, to win this battle.
Yes, Mr. President,
I am ready

4/21/22

I kissed you in my dreams last night
but instead of hello, it was goodbye
the fear drives me up inside
worry of losing you
but I believe you're my Abe Lincoln
and I'm your Mary Lou

BROKEN HARMONY

I'd spoil you
I'd love you for eternity
But then there you are, crawling
Crawling back to her broken harmony
Her cries for you
Her cries of abuse
To break
To tear apart
Your heart and soul
Darling, don't you see
She's not the one for you
You are the one for me
And I am the one to fix your heart
And sew together the pieces of your soul
Darling, don't you see
Nothing will fix her insanity
Don't you see what these drugs do
These chemicals are deadly
The choices
The disease
They're all an abomination of sadness and broken hearts
Blood
Tears
Torn veins
Honey, all I see there is sadness
And all I see here is joy
All I see there is survival
And all I see here is love
So come back to me baby

See what I've got in store
Because I'll love you and care for you
Like she never did before

11/22/21

She said who will save your soul
For I know the devil never would
Who will save you from overdose
I know I have moved on
And I know, I know you're struggling, dear
But heroin isn't the answer I want to hear
I want to hear you laugh and cry and scream and shout
I want you to feel
So don't numb the pain no more, my sweet
For time will only heal

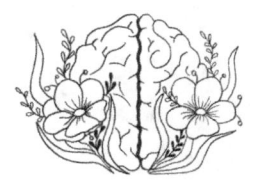

27 CLUB

We're sadistic
We're twisted
We're insane
Never again will your love be on my brain
Welcome to the 27 club, darling
Enjoy your stay
You won't have much to drink
But you have a lot to pay
You will have to pay your dues
And you have to see how you're uncool
Welcome to the 27 club, darling
Throw that white lighter away

MY KING

I was lost in your soul
your soft kiss brought me to pure bliss
I held your hand all night and we didn't let go til we
woke
it was a beautiful masterpiece
our love is a kaleidoscope of stardust
the universe hears our sighs
and our voices collide
I look into your eyes deeply
you grab my face
you are mine
I love the way you are spontaneous
and how everything seems to work in our favor
thank you for an evening of beauty
you are now my king

LOKI

I fear your snake eyes
you have damaged my soul
my body
my kidneys
my insides are failing
you are the evil in the deepest depths of hell
the one evil the universe fears
and you found me
tricked me
possessed me
I was gone
my soul depleted
but now I have risen above thee
and my spirit shines with clarity
everything is going to be okay

ANXIETY

there's a lump in my chest
a stain in my throat
the pit of my stomach is deep and dreadful
there's no more tears to cry
I am numb
pained
broken
my soul aches for joy
but I don't know if I will ever achieve such a goal

IF YOU NEED HELP:

988 Suicide and Crisis Lifeline
988

To Write Love On Her Arms
twloha.com

National Association of Anorexia Nervosa & Associated Disorders
888-375-7767

Anxiety Hotline
866-903-3787

Crisis Text Line
741741

SAHMHSA's National Helpline
(Substance Abuse and Mental Health
Services Administration)
1-800-622-HELP

Elabeth Cooney found the beauty of the written word during her formative teen years, and she has not put her pen down since. While going through a rough period dealing with a long-term mental health crisis she relied on her words to work through what she was going through. Those words became healing. Now, she relies on writing, self-care, medication, and therapy to keep her going. Now in college to study psychology, she hopes her poetry can help others going through the same thing, as well as those who have loved ones who are learning to cope with their own challenges.

Wild Ink Publishing

Wild Ink Publishing is new to the publishing industry, which means we are able to showcase some of the brightest wordsmiths by unleashing the shackles that usually stop people from publishing traditionally.

wild-ink-publishing.com

www.ingramcontent.com/pod-product-compliance
Lightning Source LLC
Chambersburg PA
CBHW070936120626
46546CB00004B/1425